For the Love of Peanuts!

Charles M. Schulz

Selected cartoons from
Good Grief, More Peanuts! Vol. II

CORONET BOOKS
Hodder Fawcett, London

First published by Fawcett Publications Inc., New York

Coronet edition 1967
Sixteenth impression 1978

Printed in Great Britain for Hodder
Fawcett Ltd., Mill Road, Dunton Green,
Sevenoaks, Kent (Editorial Office:
47 Bedford Square, London, WC1 3DP) by
C. Nicholls & Company Ltd
The Philips Park Press, Manchester

ISBN 0 340 02710 X

SCHULZ

THUMP THUMP THUMP THUMP

WHAPETY WHAPETY
WHAPETY WHAPETY
WHAP

RATS

YOU MAKE
ME NERVOUS
SNOOPY..

WHAPETY WHAPETY WHAPETY
WHAPETY WHAP

KLUNK!

SCHULZ

RIP!

SCHULZ

THE WONDERFUL WORLD OF PEANUTS

Numbers 1-25 and all the above Peanuts titles are available at your local bookshop or newsagent, or can be ordered direct from the publisher. Just tick the titles you want and fill in the form below.
Prices and availability subject to change without notice.

CORONET BOOKS, P.O. Box 11, Falmouth, Cornwall.
Please send cheque or postal order, and allow the following for postage and packing:
U.K.—One book 22p plus 10p per copy for each additional book ordered, up to a maximum of 82p.
B.F.P.O. and EIRE—22p for the first book plus 10p per copy for the next 6 books, thereafter 4p per book.

OTHER OVERSEAS CUSTOMERS—30p for the first book and 10p per copy for each additional book.

Name ....

Address ....

....